Parkour

The Complete Guide To Parkour and Freerunning For Beginners

JASON JONES

ISBN-13: 978-1514831236
ISBN-10: 1514831236

CONTENTS

PARKOUR

PARKOUR

SO YOU WANT TO LEARN PARKOUR?

So you've seen some videos on YouTube where these guys are running across rooftops, bounding from one building to the next in a style you might only have seen before in the movies. Their movements are fluent and they seem to have no fear of trying to jump a 10 foot gap between buildings while doing a couple fancy tricks here and there, and this has been peaking your curiosity to no end. How do they do that?

What you have witnessed is a running style commonly known as Parkour or Free Running and it is an increasingly popular sport in recent decades. While these two styles are extremely similar they are actually two different sports when you take a look at the history of Parkour.

This is a sport that requires extreme mental focus and physical strength, but it is also a sport that anyone who wants to put their mind to can learn! You don't need any special equipment to get started either – but that doesn't mean it's easy to do.

If you are interested in becoming a traceur (someone who utilizes, studies and practices Parkour) then this book is the ultimate starting point for you. We will go through the history of Parkour and how it became so popular as well as the differences between traditional Parkour and Free Running.

Once you know how Parkour and Free Running came to be the popular sport it is today, we will start discussing training exercises, techniques, movements, physical training and more to get you on your way to becoming an experienced traceur.

The aim of this book is get a complete beginner up and running (pun intended!) in the basic elements of Parkour. This book will help to give you the confidence and basic skills you need to start participating in the sport. Don't stop here! I recommend joining a local Parkour or

Freerunning club and meet people that have been doing it for years. This will catapult your learning to the next level. Absorb as much information as you can. Read books and articles, watch clips, and most importantly, keep training!

I hope you enjoy this sport as much as I have. We plenty of points to cover so let's get started!

PARKOUR AND FREE RUNNING: HOW THEY STARTED AND WHAT MAKES THE DIFFERENCE

The simplest definition of Parkour is the ability to move quickly and efficiently from one destination to another, using the most direct route with the ability to combat any obstacles along the way.

A Brief History of Parkour

The basic concept of Parkour was originally developed early in the 1900s by the French military. A French naval officer by the name of Georges Hebert was the first to bring the idea to the table after taking note of the efficiency and agility of movement by the people of the French Caribbean Island of Martinique. They called the style "parcours du combatant" which translates to "the path of the warrior".

While he brought the early concept to training the French military, the person who is widely known to have come up with the concept of modern Parkour was David Belle. Belle learned the basics of the French military training due to his father who completed training with the French military in the 1950's. Belle was also trained in martial arts and gymnastics as well as the philosophical training that had become a standard part of French military training.

From there he adapted his techniques of mental discipline and physical strength to develop what we know today as Parkour.

Along with Belle's best friend Sabastian Foucan the first group of traceurs were born. They called their group Yamikazi and with their unique talents they quickly grew a large following, which would include Luc Besson, a filmmaker. Besson ended up creating a film called *The*

Yamikazi, which greatly contributed to the growth in popularity of Parkour.

It was not too long after this film came out that Belle and Foucan went their separate ways, with Belle still practicing Parkour and Foucan venturing off into what would become modern day free running.

While the original traceurs went in their own direction, they all still practice some form of what originated as parcours du combatant.

Also, if we wanted to get really technical, Foucan once stated that when our ancestors were chased by game or predators, they were practicing Parkour – the ability to move quickly and efficiently from one destination to another as safely as possible. For accuracies sake though, we will stick to calling David Belle the father of Parkour as it is known today.

What Makes Parkour Different from Free Running?

Parkour and Free Running took a split when David Belle and Sebastian Foucan no longer saw eye to eye about their styles. Belle stood by the fact that Parkour was strictly about efficiency in running, by using a combination of mental focus and physical strength. Foucan felt that it should also be a form of self-expression, allowing creative moves that may not be necessary to become a part of the practice. From this point on, David Belle continued to practice Parkour and Sebastian Foucan went his own way to practice Free Running.

Prior to taking their split, there was a documentary made about Parkour called Jump London. Foucan originally used the term Free Running as sort of an English translation of Parkour. Not long after this movie was created did the phenomenon start to grow around the world.

Belle said that the purpose behind Parkour was to become efficient in case of emergency. Foucan preferred to look at it as a way to express your creative and artistic nature through movement. Over the years, these two styles have become confused and mixed. People will use the words Parkour and Freerunning interchangeably as though they are one art, which is far from the truth. I've even used both terms in the name of this book, as it's targeted for beginners who don't understand the difference between the two styles.

There are a few very important key differences between Parkour and Free Running. Parkour is the ability to take the most direct route from one place to another in the most efficient way possible. This practice would be great for any emergency situation. Parkour moves are still widely based on the original style learned by the French military in the 50's.

The style of Parkour relies heavily on vaulting over walls, landing on narrow spaces, rolling and even hanging. This practice is very focused on self-improvement, individual mental discipline and physical strength as well as a connection between the body and mind. Parkour is never meant to be a competitive sport, but more of a training technique for the body and mind.

On the other hand, Free Running is more of an artistic way to express yourself as you move through your environment with no limitation on movements. Adding in extra moves for style can actually slow you down, meaning it is not exactly a practical way to practice Parkour. Free Running also may be practiced in both urban and natural settings while Parkour is generally in an urban setting.

While Parkour is mostly quick and simple moves that help you get by different obstacles, Free Running allows more of a creative touch. Common moves used in Free Running include flips, spins and many other theatrical tricks. With a creative enough imagination and a disciplined enough Free Running, almost anything is possible.

Though the terms are generally mixed up these days for a lack of true understanding, it is best to keep them in their respective places. While you can incorporate the basics of Parkour into Free Running, you cannot incorporate Free Running into Parkour.

Why You Should Practice Parkour (or Free Running)

There are a multitude of reasons you should consider practicing parkour, from physical to the psychological health benefits. The best part of all is that anyone can practice parkour at some level. Around the world parkour is now practiced by people of all ages ranging from children of 6-8 years old to senior citizens. You do not have to jump large gaps and leap over tall fences to be practicing parkour – there really is a lot more to it than that.

Let's explore some of the benefits you might find from taking part in this sport.

The Physical Benefits

When you practice parkour, you are going to be training your entire body as well as your mind. Whether you are in shape or not at the start, after a couple months of training, you will be much more physically fit overall. People even claim to reap the benefits of parkour as early as a week or two into training – and it's because they are giving their entire body a workout it has needed.

As a traceur you will regularly be working out every part of your body. Your workout will entail speed, strength, power, agility, cardio, stamina, endurance, and balance, which cover all the main physical attributes. Practicing parkour develops muscle strength in your entire body over time. You will increase stamina and endurance, being able to run farther and for much longer periods of time. You will learn to find your center, improve your balance and your coordination over all.

You only have to practice at your comfort level when taking part in parkour. You should never attempt a jump or vault you are not confident you can accomplish safely – this means knowing your limits. As you train, you'll get stronger and become more accomplished at identifying what you're physically capable of.

Most traceurs will develop lean muscle tissue. If you join a club, which I recommend or watch clips on YouTube you'll see the experienced athletes have low body fat percentage, with well defined abs, arms and legs. You're also learning functional movements that transfer into numerous physical activities.

The Psychological Benefits

Not only is parkour amazing to increase your overall physical health, it is extremely good for your mental health as well. While you may be thinking, well, of course it does, all exercise helps your mental health, but this is not the only reason parkour is so great for your mental state.

When training parkour you need to learn how to break down different movements and situations in the blink of an eye. At first, it will take some time to be able to execute a vault over a fence with a running start. You might miss, you might not have great form, but that will all come with time, practice and patience. The thing you must realize here is that you are speeding up the connection between your brain and your body – making everything happen at a split-second notice.

You need to be able to clear your mind of your daily stressors and focus on exactly what you are trying to do in order to achieve your goal. Parkour requires you to think creatively and quickly, enhancing problem solving skills (which can be transferred into other day to day activities and situations). This takes quite a bit of practice and staying focused can be even more difficult. In time though, that connection will work on rapid fire and you will be able to face a variety of obstacles in a single run without hesitation.

Boosts Confidence and Create Lasting Friendships

Along with the traditional outlook on benefits of Parkour as mentioned above, there are many additional benefits. The two biggest of which are the ability to boost confidence and create lasting friendships. This is really true of any sport, but the difference with Parkour is that it is not any other sport, but rather a lifestyle if you will. Traceurs are different from other athletes in that parkour is not meant to be a competition.

It is understandable that different people will perform at different skill levels and that is perfectly acceptable with parkour, unlike so many other sports today. When you join a community of traceurs, you will be joining a group of people who are coming together to enjoy one common goal – to improve their skills and be the best they can be.

In parkour, every small accomplishment is a confidence booster – especially when you have a group of people telling you how awesome your improvements have been! If you could barely handle a roll at the beginning of the day, or week and you finally perfect it, you're going to feel a great sense of achievement and satisfaction. This is great for self-esteem and is one of the things that keeps traceurs training day after day.

If you have wanted a way to start getting in shape, where people will accept you at any fitness and skill level then parkour may be perfect for you. Soon you will be part of a group of people who are all there to support one another in the goals of complete mental and physical health.

It's Fun and Anyone Can Join In

As mentioned earlier, you can be any age or fitness level to enjoy practicing parkour – it will just be at a different level than someone else. Some people who may be afraid of heights would prefer to stick to ground level obstacles, while those feeling more adventurous may want to sprint across rooftops.

The thing to remember is, that as long as you are improving your physical and mental strength and practicing your ability to overcome obstacles in order to get from one place to another in the most effective way, you are practicing parkour!

One of the most important things to remember is to always keep improving. If you've nailed one move, try a new one the next day. Try going to a new location, finding a new route or change up your routine so that you are constantly developing your skills, rather than repeating ones you have already perfected.

I would say that this is the biggest draw for me personally. I've been practicing the sport for over 5 years now, and although I feel I've reached a good level, there's always more things for me to learn and practice. I'm constantly trying to get better at the same basic techniques, whilst learning new ones every few weeks.

ALWAYS PRACTICE SAFE PARKOUR

Parkour is not meant to be a dangerous sport – quite the opposite, the idea behind parkour is to move from one place to the next in the most efficient and safe way possible. That doesn't mean that jumping over a 10 foot gap is easy or safe for that matter, it just means that those traceurs have already prepared themselves to handle that kind of a jump.

The best way to practice parkour is to always be as safe as you possibly can. If you are not 100% sure that you are going to make a jump, just don't do it. It's as simple as that. It's not worth it.

You will want to start off small and totally on the ground. You've probably seen the YouTube videos of people jumping from building to building and running up walls, hanging off of one fire escape and swinging their body to the next place but you can't just go out and do it. Take your time, start slow and prepare your body and your mind for the task at hand.

David Belle and Sebastian Foucan both stated that Parkour (and free running) are not a typical sport. You should not be practicing Parkour so you have a way to show off, but because you want to prepare your body to be ready for anything. It's a mental discipline that is not easy to learn and will take lots of time, patience and practice but in the end you will be able to transfer the same sort of mental clarity used to find the most efficient path to overcoming all your problems, not just how to get from one place to another.

How to Safely Learn Parkour

You should always start off at ground level and work your way up to bigger challenges. The idea is to perfect a movement before moving on to another more difficult movement. There is a saying that goes, practices doesn't make perfect, perfect practice makes perfect. Basically, this means that for every time you get something wrong, you have to get it right twice that many times for it to have really stuck in your brain.

I like to use an 80% benchmark. If I did a movement 10 times in a row, I should be able to do it to a high standard at least 8 out of 10 times. If I'm only getting it right every other time, I need to practice more.

It is a long process, but like I said, parkour isn't easy – but after 50 solid landings, you should be pretty confident to move up to a slightly higher surface to jump from and still be able to make a solid landing. You should now attempt this jump as many times as needed in the same fashion before moving forward to another more difficult level.

Diligence and patience are keys to successfully practicing parkour. You need to be prepared to spend hours and hours on a single move in order to perfect it and move on. If you are not the most physically fit before starting parkour, you may want to start with strength training as well as on the ground practice so that your body is better prepared to handle the intense workout of parkour. I'll discus physical training later in the book.

Parkour Equipment and Gear

One of the best things about Parkour is the fact that you need very little equipment to practice and perform parkour moves. There are people who even practice barefoot or in minimalist shoes and that is it – but this should be reserved for more advanced traceurs. Here's a list of the basic equipment considerations.

Shoes

Your shoes are the most important part of preparing to start practicing parkour. You will want to get a pair of shoes that are comfortable, easy to move in and have thin padding or a slim sole. The thinner shoes will encourage you to land softly and will strengthen your ankle stability. A classic example I see in my local club is the Dunlop Volleys.

16

Alternatively, a basic running shoe will do just fine if you're starting out. They'll last longer, but they're thicker sole might lead to a little more complacency when landing.

If you have a little more money to spend you could look into five finger shoes or parkour specific trainers, which are getting more popular now.

Either way, you will want to make sure that your shoes fit right and they are not loose in the heel or toe areas as this can affect your ability to run, jump and land properly.

Clothing

Mostly, you will want to wear loose fitting clothing that allows free and easy movement. This will allow you to easily conduct the movements - though some will argue that more form fitting clothes are best so they do not catch on anything. If you are just starting out, a loose pair of shorts and a t-shirt will be just fine since most of your training will be on the ground. As you hone your skills however and start to do more advanced moves, you may agree with others that form fitting clothes meet your needs better. Overall, as long as you are comfortable and able to move freely without any restrictions, then you are wearing the right clothing for parkour.

Gloves

Wearing gloves is often a debate among traceurs. Ideally, your hands will form calluses, making it easier to grip and hold your own body weight and wearing gloves can prevent the formation of these calluses. If you do choose to wear gloves, then you should make sure that the fingers have been cut in order to maintain a solid grip. Also, wearing gloves is not always efficient in rain or wet conditions, so depending on the weather and where you a practicing you may not want to be wearing gloves anyway. I'm a little 'old skool' and like to go bare hands, but I know experience traceurs that use gloves a lot of the time. It's down to you, but be careful and consider the lack of grip you may have wearing

17

them.

Miscellaneous Items

There is no need for extra equipment when practicing parkour. Everything is done with simple body movements and should require nothing but you and the environment in which you are practicing. On the other hand, it is important to keep your I.D. on you at all times. This is simply because accidents do happen – and if you do get hurt, you want the emergency help to be able to identify who you are so they can get you the proper treatment.

When it comes to everyday items like your phone and keys, these can become hazardous if carried in a pocket while practicing parkour. Many a phone screen has been demolished because someone landed on it while practicing a new jump and keys could end up stabbing you in the leg. It is best to keep these things in a backpack nearby or in a pouch or sling that is designed for traceurs. These pouches are meant to effectively hold the bare essentials and stay close to your body as to not affect your movements.

Let people know where you're training, and ideally train with others. I rarely train alone on movements and techniques. If you don't know anyone that's interested in trying it out, show them a clip on YouTube, share details in this book, or join a club.

BALANCING THE BASICS

Balancing is one of the most important skills to refine if you plan on practicing parkour. Every move in parkour requires extremely good balance. If you don't already have very good balance, then it might be one of the first things you are going to want to improve on. There are many different ways to increase your balance and it is simply not true that coordination and balance are talents we are born with, they simply come more naturally to some than others, and like any skill, it can be learned through practice. Let's have a look at some exercises that will help improve your balance.

Rail Exercises

These exercises are great for your balance and you can do them anywhere there is a railing. You could use a low to the ground balance beam at a playground if you are unsure and looking for a little more stability but a round, tube like bar (such as a handrail) is definitely preferred for these exercises.

Rail Walk

This doesn't require much description. Find a rail (or a wall), stand up tall, keep your arms out wide to balance your weight, and walk across it. To increase the difficulty, find a thinner rail or wall and then gradually start increasing the height when you feel more confident.

Rail Plank

Lift yourself onto the railing and place your hands side by side. Make sure that you have a tight grip then extend your legs behind you until you are balancing on the tips of your toes. Your back should be straight as in a regular plank position on the ground. You're essentially doing a regular plank on a rail, but it's that much harder because you have to balance. Maintain this for around thirty seconds at a time if possible.

Three Point Balance

Get on the bar in a semi-kneeling position. Once again, your hands should be side by side and you should be sure you have a firm grip. Then you should slowly lift one foot off of the rail and attempt to hold the position. You should hold this position for about 15 seconds and if you can, switch to the other leg.

Cat Balancing

You should start just as you did for the three point balance, but with your limbs slightly more spread out. Now carefully let go and reach forward with one hand, and attempt to crawl across the railing. Walk like a cat would, nice, confident and smoothly. This one is all about distance, so aim to go as far as you can go whilst keeping your form.

With rail exercises, you will also start to conquer any fears of being off the ground. Always start with something close to the ground because falling onto cement does not feel good now or later. Once you are rather comfortable with your ability to perform these exercises with ease you should aim for something at least a couple feet off the ground.

Handstands and More

Handstands are a great way to practice balancing and it is also something you will need to master in order to properly execute certain parkour moves. It takes time and practice to be able to get a perfect handstand.

Wall Handstand

If you're training on your own, I recommend having your back to a wall, with your heels close to the wall. Now crouch down into a press up position with your heels almost touching the wall, whilst the rest of your body is out perpendicular to it. Once you're in the press up position, start walking (with your arms) backwards towards the wall and use your legs to climb up the wall. Go as high as you're comfortable to do so, hold for a set period (somewhere between 10 and 60 seconds), and then walk yourself back out with your hands. You can gradually hold yourself longer over time and eventually reach a point where you're in the full handstand position next to a wall for safety.

Walking Down Stairs

With your arms first, not your legs! I love this exercise. I walk down my stairs 5-20times a day, so why not use that time to practice my upper body balance and strength. I walk down the stairs headfirst, with my arms. My body is sprawled out behind me and is always in contact with the floor throughout.

Frog Stand

Along with a traditional handstand you should also practice the Frog Stand. This is where you start off sitting as though you were a frog, with your knees up to your chest, your butt off the ground and your arms on either side in front of you. From this position you should lean forward and raise your body upwards while holding the position so your feet come off the ground. Try holding it for 5-10 seconds initially, and eventually build up to holding it 30-60 seconds.

After around three years of training, I was able to combine a Frog Stand up into a handstand, but **I do not recommend you trying this now**. I say it not to impress you, but to show what's possible with practice. I couldn't even hold a Frog Stand when I first started.

A handstand of any sort is not only an excellent form of balance training, but it is also great strength training. It will be exercises like these and pull-ups that will help you to hang and swing from one place to another with ease later on, and you'll notice that your physique will start to change with it.

Improving your balance will help you to smoothly pull off any parkour move you may come across. Starting with the basics is the best way to build yourself up both physically and mentally for the challenge ahead. Balance takes patience and persistence to improve, but once you do there is a world of opportunities out there for you in parkour training.

Some of these techniques, like cat balancing, for example, are far more difficult than others. When you can successfully cat balance and crawl for more than a few feet you are ready for a little more advanced parkour training. Aim to improve on one or more of these techniques at a time. Shoot for the 80% success benchmark and stick with it, in the end it will be well worth the time you put in I promise.

LONG RANGE MOVEMENT

There are three different forms of typical long range movement when it comes to parkour. Those would be running, climbing, hanging/swinging. While all the individual movements such as the parkour roll and the Kong vault are used to aid you in getting from place to place, these four things will make up a good portion of your run and are therefore a great place to start.

Running

Seeing as running was even implemented into the adaption to parkour, free running, is seems logical that you have to be prepared to run – a lot. Then again, a lot doesn't necessarily begin to cover it. You see, once you get started on the journey of learning parkour and becoming a skilled traceur, all you might want to do is run.

Start conditioning for this right away by going for regular runs every week and slowly increase either the distance or the speed you run. I recommend somewhere between 3-5 times a week as a beginner. Even if it's to your local park and back where you do parkour. You'll start to lose body fat and build stamina at the same time. It will be beneficial when you first start adding extra moves in because you will not tire out as quickly as someone who does not run regularly.

Climbing

There are a couple of different ways you may find yourself climbing in parkour. You may be climbing a set of stairs or a fire escape, which could be simple enough. You can practice this right away by going to the local high school football stadium and running up and down the stadium steps. This is actually a great way to build your endurance for climbing for long periods of time.

You may also find yourself climbing up walls, something that you may not have thought you were capable of. This takes much more practice and should not be attempted until you are well prepared for it, but will eventually be an extremely commonly used movement in your practices. I recommend trying to climb with your legs first – running up steps, and then building in upper body climbing, like pulling yourself up over walls or rails.

Hanging & Swinging

You will eventually want to be able to hold your body weight with just your arms. This is on a wall or a rail. This is where hanging comes in – this can happen quite often in parkour and you need to be ready for it. The best way to condition your muscles for this sort of activity is to do pull-ups or find something that will support your bodyweight, with collapsing, which takes your feet off the ground. A climbing frame or monkey bars at your local kid's park is perfect.

Once you've practiced hanging from bars or walls and you feel more comfortable doing so, you can start experimenting with body swings on a set of monkey bars. Propel your body forward with the momentum from your feet. You generate the most force from the point furthest from your hands! Allow yourself to swing from one bar to another, sort of Tarzan vine swinging style, but with bars instead of vines. If you're feeling more adventurous, you can find some low level tree branches and really take on the Tarzan persona.

For all of these different types of movement you will want to start off easy and work your way up to the more challenging. Only go as far as you can, if your body is saying it needs rest, then listen. You will be more at risk for injuries if you do not give your body the rest it deserves. The beginning is all about building strength, endurance and stamina.

MOVEMENTS IN PARKOUR

If you've watched any videos online or seen anyone practicing parkour before, then you are well aware that there are several moves that are clearly defined as parkour movements. These are going to be the most efficient ways for you to move beyond obstacles that may be on your path and blocking the quickest route to where you want to be.

Some of these moves include jumping, vaulting, rolling and landing. Different variants of these moves will make up your "library" of moves you can turn to while pursuing an actual parkour run. This chapter is going to compile all the different moves in parkour, starting from the first ones you should learn in order to prepare yourself to do more difficult moves in the future.

Landings

The two most important moves any traceur needs to learn are the Basic Landing and the Parkour Roll. These are the two landings that you need to know in order to safely land after any jump you make.

The Basic Landing

To properly execute the Basic Landing you should start your practices at ground level. With proper technique you should be able to:

- Land on the balls of your feet.
- Don't let your knees bend more than 90 degrees.
- Keep your back straight.

To practice this, you can simply jump forward as far as you can and practice landing with the proper form. Landing on the balls of your feet will help to absorb the impact evenly. Having shoes with a thinner sole should help with this. Keeping your knees at 90 degrees and no further can prevent injury to the joint and keeping your back straight not only reduces injury but it also helps you to balance upon landing.

This landing is perfect for many close to the ground jumps – Eg. From a picnic table or a short ledge. You should be confident in your ability to execute this landing perfectly from the ground before you can move on to higher platforms.

There is another step to this landing that is extremely helpful when it comes to making a landing from a higher level. It is especially effective when you are running before a jump and want to take off again right after you land.

The final step adds in the use of your hands. When you land this way, you will want to lean forward with your arms out in front of you, allowing your hands to absorb a portion of the landing. Once you've landed with your hands, you can push yourself up and forward right back into a run again. This is a little more complicated to get a handle on than simply landing on your feet, so practice this move from the ground several times over before attempting this from a running jump off of something. To help, imagine yourself as Spiderman, seriously. He lands with his feet first and then follows up with his hands to support. You don't need to get spandex or a facemask, but the web shooter would go a long way.

The Parkour Roll

This particular technique is arguably the most important move for you to learn in all of parkour. The roll allows you to land safely from any height by evenly distributing and absorbing the impact throughout your body. There are a few different ways to go about entering a parkour roll but each will give you the desired effect and movement. We will discuss three of the easiest and most common ways to execute a proper parkour roll.

Table Top Roll

The "Table Top" version of the parkour roll starts with you on all fours with your legs about shoulder width apart. Your hands should be out in front of you making a diamond shape with your thumb and index fingers

– extend towards the opposite shoulder of the one you plan to roll over.

You should then slowly tuck the arm you plan to roll over inwards towards your body and push your body forwards to roll over your shoulder. When you come out of the roll you will roll over the opposite hip of the shoulder you started the roll with.

One leg will remain tucked in after the roll and the other will come forward for the landing, giving you the ability to push off the ground and keep moving.

In the three examples below, let's assume you plan to roll over your right shoulder.

- Start with your knees shoulder width apart and your hands out in front of you.
- Lean towards your left with your hands on the ground creating a diamond with your thumb and index fingers.
- Slowly lean forward into the roll while tucking your right elbow down and then inwards towards your body.
- Your left leg should remain tucked in as you roll over your left hip.
- You should exit the roll with your right leg landing in front (which when you have more momentum will allow you to push up and into a run).

Split Leg

The "Split Leg" variant of the roll differs in the way you start the roll. Rather than on all fours as you are in the Table Top technique, for the Split Leg you will start upright, kneeling with the leg up on the side of the shoulder you plan to roll over. So if you plan to roll over your right shoulder, you right leg should be up.

From this position you would simply push yourself forward into the roll, tucking in your shoulder to roll over and across your back to the opposite hip. You should come out of the roll in the same manner as you did in the Table Top.

- Start in a kneeling position. The leg that is up should be your right leg, bent at no more than a 90 degree angle.
- Lean forward with your body using that leg to move you into the roll, over your right shoulder and across your back to your left hip.
- You should exit the roll with your right leg in front prepared to push off and continue a run.

Arm Thread

The "Arm Thread" technique is almost the exact same as the Table Top technique. The only change you are going to make is in the first couple of movements. If you are having trouble with rolling diagonally across you're your back or the tucking your elbow in, this may be a better option for you.

You start out the roll exactly as you did before, but rather than tucking your elbow in, you will take your arm and thread it through the space between your arm and your leg. This allows your body to easily roll in a diagonal movement over your shoulder across your back and to the opposite hip.

- Start with your knees shoulder width apart and your hands out in front of you.
- As you lean your body forward, thread your right arm through the space between your left arm and leg.
- Your left leg should remain tucked in as you roll across your back and over your left hip.
- You should exit the roll with your right leg landing in front (which when you have more momentum will allow you to push up and into a run).

These are all effective ways to start the Rolling technique. Once you're performing the roll correctly at least 80% of the time you can start practicing from a standing position.

This starts to add momentum to your roll. Once you feel confident with your standing start (achieving the 80% benchmark), try jumping into the roll. (Tip – Don't forget to use the basic landing technique in jumps and always land on the balls of your feet)

Jumping

One of the things that seems to draw attention to parkour more than any vault, is the jumps. It's impressive to watch someone clear a 10 foot gap between buildings and sticking the landing perfectly, before moving on. It takes a lot of practice to be able to clear such a space in a single jump and land perfectly, but I've seen many people learn this technique from scratch and so can you.

The Precision Jump

This is the jump you are going to want to perfect in order to jump large gaps in the future. I would encourage you to work on the technique of this jump to a stage where you feel 100% confident before try to increase the distance of it. The distance will come with practice, but focus on your technique right from the start.

How to perform the precision jump:

- Stand with your feet about shoulder width apart and your arms out straight in front of you.
- Use your legs and arms to create momentum by squatting down and pulling your arms behind you, still straightened out.
- As you go to jump, lean forward and swing your arms up and push off with your legs all in one motion.
- When you land your feet should hit just below the balls of your feet.

You should start out on the ground as with any move in order to avoid injury. Pick a spot or use tape or a marker of sorts to pick the spot you want to land your jump. Proper form and landings are very important and you want to get your technique as crisp and tight as possible before you start trying to make jumps over larger stretches of empty space. As you continue to practice this jump on the floor with targets, you'll start to build awareness of how far you can jump. When you see people leaping between large gaps, it might look impressive, but they know they can clear the gap comfortably because of the practice they've put in to their technique, and the experience they've gained of knowing how far they can push themselves safely. Test yourself hundreds or even thousands of times on the ground before moving up in height.

Vaults

When you are out on a parkour run, one of the moves you will use frequently are vaults. They help you to get your body up and over obstacles such as fences, walls, railings and more. I've listed three basic vaults to get you started.

The Safety Vault

Ideally, this is the first vault technique you want to learn as it will make learning other vaults much easier, plus this is the easiest, most routine and safest vault to learn. Vaults are some of the most common movements in parkour, so it is very important that you take your time to learn the proper technique.

To do the safety vault you will need either a low to the ground ledge or railing. Your first obstacles should be no higher than your hips as a guide. This can greatly reduce risk of injury while you are learning. Once you have found a suitable place to practice, here are the steps to a successful safety vault.

How to perform a Safety Vault: (For the sake of the example we will say you are starting by lifting your right leg.)

- Place both your hands on the bar, parallel to your shoulders and about shoulder width apart.

- As you jump up to the bar lift your right leg up onto the bar to the side of your body.
- Now you are going to pull your other leg up and over the bar between your right leg and left arm.
- Your right arm should move upwards as you move you your leg through.

This should end up being one single motion when it's done properly. Don't forget to move your arm when you move your second leg, and be careful not to catch your foot or shin on the railing instead of going over. These can cause you to fall, which is why starting from a low-to-the-ground ledge or railing is best when you first start attempting the safety vault.

Start slow, as though you are walking over the railing. Once you are comfortable, start working your way up by giving yourself more momentum with a jump into it from a standing position. From there, try giving it a go with a short run before you vault. This is the best way to work your way up to being ready for some of the more advanced vaulting techniques.

The Turn Vault

The Turn Vault allows you to go over a ledge, railing or similar and find yourself in a "cat position" with the freedom to keep forward momentum moving with a single move. This is one of the more common vaults used and it's important for beginning traceurs to learn.

How to perform a Turn Vault: (For this example going over to the right side and turning towards your left shoulder.)

- You will want your left hand to grip the bar in an underhand position and your right hand to hold an overhand position (like a left-hander would grip a baseball bat).

- Keeping your arms straight and your feet about shoulder width apart you should lower your hips and hold yourself up with your arms keeping them straight.
- Jump into the vault and lift your hips, as you start to rotate tuck your legs into your body and extend for the landing.
- Turn your body towards your left shoulder and allow your left hand to rotate to where it is now over the railing.
- Your other arm will let go and rotate with your body, then grip the rail again once you are facing the railing.
- Land gently on the balls of your feet, allowing your body to slowly lower into the cat position you started in.

One of the trickiest parts of getting this move right is balance. This can be controlled better by having your supporting arm (in this example – left arm) be the center point of your body, balancing over it. Practice this move slowly the first couple of times and be sure you can lift your body high enough to clear the railing. Once you are feeling comfortable with this, start emphasizing your jump or even taking a running start from a few feet away. Eventually, this series of movements should look and feel like one fluid movement.

The Kong Vault

This is one of the more advanced vaults, but it is also one of the most useful vaults you are going to learn. The Kong vault is extremely good for getting over longer obstacles and gaining distance, rather than for picking up speed. The Kong Vault is also known as the Monkey Vault and Cat Pass, but is most often referred to as the Kong.

How to perform the Kong Vault:

- Jump towards the rail, table, wall or ledge you wish to vault over – your hands should land about shoulder width apart if not a little closer together, palms facing down.
- Then tuck your knees in close to your chest and thread them through your arms and over the ledge.

- You should use your arms to propel your body forward, gaining as much distance as possible.
- You should land on the balls of your feet to absorb the impact and maintain momentum.

To work your way up to being able to properly perform a Kong Vault you should start on the ground, practicing the movement of your legs passing through your arms. This will help prepare you to avoid clipping your feet or legs on a ledge or anything of the sort. Once you are comfortable on the ground, start with a comfortable obstacle that is close to the ground before moving up.

This move can also be done one handed (as can many vaults) once the right level of coordination and strength have been achieved. As you improve with vaults you will want to learn to go over higher and more advanced obstacles and that is fine. Just always remember to implement proper landings for the height from which you will be vaulting, dropping or jumping.

The Lazy Vault

The Lazy Vault doesn't take as much strength and practice as the Kong Vault – hence the name. This move is great for changing directions or making drops from one level down to another. When it comes to learning the vaults this is one of the easier ones for beginners in parkour.

How to perform the Lazy Vault: (assuming you use your right arm for stability)

- Grip the railing with your right hand in the overhand position.
- Use the momentum of running to move your body forward and swing your legs and hips up and over the railing, inside leg first with the rest of your body following.
- Your free hand should grip the railing in the opposite direction to help you to control your direction.

- You should land on the part of your foot just below the ball of your foot. The first leg over is the leg you should land on first – unless you are going to experience a drop, in which case you should use the basic landing.

When practicing the Lazy Vault you should start off with only a couple of steps running into the move and use a ledge closer to the ground. Once you have confidently accomplished the Lazy Vault at a lower ledge you can move up to a railing and maybe a longer running start. Eventually you should practice a Lazy Vault that will end in a drop and basic landing.

The Speed Vault

The Speed Vault is really a variation of the Safety Vault. The biggest differences between the two moves is that the Speed Vault is done one handed and while running at top speed. It can be used to clear both small railings and large objects like cars. Tackle this technique after you've gained confidence in the others. When you are successful at any of the other vaults, learning this particular one should only be a matter of speed and a little practice.

How to perform a Speed Vault: (assuming you use your right arm for stability)

- As you are coming up to the railing reach out and grip the railing in an overhand position.
- Use your speed to propel your body up and over the obstacle, with your legs out to the side.
- You should land on the balls of your feet or just below that, one foot right after the other in order to keep your momentum and speed.

This move is great when you find yourself with a sudden obstacle that you simply need to get past. You can work your way up to this move by practicing on a low-to-the-ground railing or ledge and moving up to higher obstacles from there. You can also start with a couple of steps into the move until you are comfortable attempting the vault at a full run.

The Wall Run

Have you ever seen someone seemingly run up a wall with ease, managing to reach the top of the wall and pulling themselves over? This is a more advanced and very handy parkour movement to learn and will highly increase the efficiency of your run.

The wall run is difficult because you have to have a pair of shoes with great grip, just the right speed and momentum to propel your body up the wall. It will take a lot of practice and patience but will be well worth it when you need this move later on.

How to perform a Wall Run:

- Run at the wall with a powerful but still semi-light jog.
- Your foot will hit the wall on the balls of your foot – your body should be at roughly a 90 degree angle – use that foot to jump and push yourself upward.
- Reach out with the hand opposite of the foot that first hit the wall and catch the top of the wall.
- Start in a hanging position then carefully pull your body over the wall.

You can use the same basic movement to use a wall to change direction. Instead of jumping upward to grab the top of the wall, you should use that first foot hitting the wall to help you change direction and keep momentum.

How the Moves Make-Up Parkour

This was not a full list of all the moves throughout parkour, but these are some of the moves that are used most often and perfect for beginners. Eventually, when you have perfected enough of these moves you will be prepared to go for an entire parkour run where you will meet many obstacles requiring you to execute these moves on a moment's notice.

You may come across several different chances to use a Speed Vault,

Kong Vault as well as your Precision Jump and maybe even the Wall Run all in one outing. You may find yourself using a mixture of the basic landing, the parkour roll and eventually the cat position, after a mixture of vaults drops and jumps. This is why it is so important to get your basic landing and parkour roll down right from the start – these are going to be the safest ways to land until you learn more advanced techniques.

Once your body and mind are sure of how to complete the move, in any scenario, on any terrain and with only a split second to make a decision on which move to use, then it is time to start adding runs into your training mix.

When you've successfully trained each of these moves from a standing or slow running start, you should be cautious and stick close to the ground for the first few runs. If you make any mistakes, there is much less chance of injury. Once you are feeling comfortable and confident with a full run on the ground you can consider moving up to bigger obstacles including buildings and more.

CONDITIONING YOUR BODY FOR PARKOUR

Depending on your current level of athleticism and strength some of these workouts may be a little tough at first. The best thing you can do is to keep at it and start with smaller sets of reps and add more reps to each set and increase the number of sets to your workout as you get stronger.

Along with all the basic moves that you will be learning and practicing, here is a list of exercises that will help you to build strength in your arms, legs and core which will dramatically increase your parkour ability.

Pull-Ups

These will increase your arm strength, grip strength and your core strength. Start with a standard pull-up with your hands gripping the bar in the other head position and pulling your body upward so your chin is over the height of the bar. Do 10 reps minimally per set when you start out. If you cannot do a full set, do 10 jumping pull ups where you use your legs to leap up to the bar and use the momentum to pull you up. If these are too difficult, try doing pull ups whilst having you feet in contact with the ground.

Once you have gotten the hang of the pull-up in an underhand position, turn your hands around to grip the bar in an overhand position which will work a slightly different muscle group. Ultimately, you should be able to do at least two sets of 10 with each hand placement in one workout.

Another great way to use pull-up's for strength training is to hold yourself up in the pull up position, where you have pulled your chin up to the bar level, now hold this position for as long as possible. Repeat at least 2 to 5 times in a day, holding for as long as you can – aim for 30+ seconds at a time if you can.

I recommend doing pull ups 2 to 3 times a week. Make sure you allow rest days in between sessions for your muscles to recover, this is when they grow!

Squats and Box Jumps

At first you will want to perfect your form and proficiency with squats. You should do at least 10 repetitions per set with 2 to 3 sets. This will work out your upper and lower leg, butt and core muscles. With consistent training you'll be able to squat up to 50, 100 or even 200 reps at a time.

Eventually you will be able to do a box jump, which is where you start in a squatting position, use your legs to jump upwards and then land silently and ease back down into the squatting position.

Ultimately, you will be able to do at least two sets of 10 box jumps as a part of your workout routine. Once you are capable of this, you should attempt a "drop squat" or "depth drop" where you basically walk off of a ledge or similar and as you use your basic landing you will also drop down into a squat.

You can take this a step further by doing a depth drop and upon landing, leap up as high as you can. This a plyometric exercise, so keep the reps and sets low – 2 to 3 sets of 3 to 5 reps is more than enough. You should not go to 'failure' in plyometric movements.

Keep lower body strength training to 2 to 3 days a week, making sure you have rest days in between.

Push Up's

Push up's will not only help strengthen your arms, upper body and core but it can also be a part of your balance training if you can get to where you can do these exercises on a rail. Start with simple push up's with 2 to 3 sets of 10. If you can't perform pull push ups, start on your knees rather than your feet. Once you can perform 3 sets of 10 reps on your knees, try building up the reps and sets on your feet.

Press up reps build up over time, and like squats, continue to practice the basic movement to 30, 50, or even 100 reps in time.

If you find press ups easy, you can put your feet on an elevated platform, like a bench, try parallel dips or even work up to handstand push ups.

For variety, you can work your way up to where you can clap while you are in the air and safely land with your hands back in position.

I recommend mixing push ups with pull ups in the same workout. The pushing and pulling movements complement each other and even act as a rest for each movement.

Quadrupedal Movement

This is the act of moving on all fours. This is a great exercise in parkour because it's not only great for strength training but also for coordination and balance. You will be on the balls of your feet and down on your hands in the "all fours" position. Then you will move your opposite foot and hand together in unison (left hand and right leg should move at the same time). Start off with walking and ease into being able to run efficiently on all fours. This is actually a move you will potentially use later in a parkour run, when you need to get across uneven terrain as well as under or through small spaces. (This is an easier version of the Cat Balance we mentioned earlier in this guide, so if you tried that and are having trouble, consider starting with ground level quadrupedal movement before advancing to Cat balancing).

I started walking around my house like this all the time. No one can see me walking around like a cat (apart from my girlfriend), I get to practice the technique more often, and the floor's nice and soft so I keep it going for longer.

Working Your Way Up to More Advanced Techniques

All of these strength training techniques use your body as the resistance, which is one of the all-time best ways to prepare for parkour. Since you are going to be lifting your body during each vault and using muscles you might not even know you have to jump and land it is really important to know how to use your own weight to your advantage.

These workouts will not only help you learn better balance and posture for your parkour movements but it will also help your muscles become strong enough throw around your body weight as though you were lighter than a feather. It takes lots of time, practice, persistence and dedication to master your own body strength and parkour is a great motivator to do so.

The freedom you feel while seemingly flying through your environment will be like no other and it will keep you wanting more and more. It is for this reason that people don't often give up on parkour, rather they look at everything as an obstacle to be overcome, no matter how long it may take them to get there.

Start with what is comfortable for you. Everyone starts out training at a different level. Some people are already fit and athletic and able to master a basic landing or safety vault in only a day or two and others can take weeks or months to be able to successfully perform these moves.

Don't be discouraged though, because the whole point of training parkour is to prepare yourself for emergency, become a better problem solver and to continuously improve your skills and abilities. Never attempt something you are not comfortable with just to impress someone else! This should be something you do for yourself, because you enjoy it and not because you feel you have to.

Practice as often as you can – most traceurs practice every day, though at first this may be too much for you. The basic workouts above, push-ups, squats, etc. should all be done at least every other day until you have built up the strength to handle longer and more frequent training sessions.

It is all about sustainability and endurance – eventually, you will be able to go for a full on run and probably run for as long as you like before getting seriously tired. This will take time to work up to however, so don't feel like you need to rush, pushing yourself to be better now. Everyone builds skills at their own pace, so find yours and be patient and persistent to get to the level you want to be at.

GET PRACTICING

After learning about how parkour got started and the differences between parkour and free running, you should have a good idea of which direction you want to go in your training. If you are hoping to have the skills you need to out-run a zombie in the apocalypse, then parkour is probably the way to go. On the other hand, if you are looking to have a creative way to exercise and express yourself at the same time, free running might be more your thing. Either way, you now have the basic knowledge you need to get started in parkour, which will only help you to transfer over to free running.

You have instructions on how to improve your balance, build your strength and endurance and even a guide to learning a few of the more popular and basic moves in parkour. All that's left is to go outside and get practicing.

If you have been imaging yourself flying over rooftops, running up walls and vaulting over cars and walls, landing with ease and continuing on in a split second, then it's time to stop imagining and make it a reality.

It will take time. It will take hard work and patience. In the end though, it will all be worth it. The mental discipline that it takes to dedicate yourself to learning parkour is incredible and it will help you in various other aspects of your life from problem solving to self-esteem and confidence.

All that's left now is to see these benefits for yourself – so before you go and watch more videos on YouTube of other people getting the thrill of practicing parkour, consider instead putting on your trainers and getting your start in the world of parkour.

Be safe and have fun!

RESOURCES ON THE WEB

There are numerous places for you to find information online about Parkour and Freerunning. Here are some of the resources I use and recommend to get you started in this sport.

Parkour History

http://www.wfpf.com/history-parkour/

http://www.discoverparkour.org/hello-world/

http://www.parkourtrain.net/parkour-history

http://parkourvisions.org/what-is-parkour/

http://learnmoreparkour.com/about-parkour/

http://parkourpedia.com/about/what-is-parkour

http://www.parkouruk.org/about/what-is-parkour/

http://www.livestrong.com/article/460811-parkour-facts/

Parkour VS Free Running

http://www.diffen.com/difference/Freerunning_vs_Parkour

http://www.parkourtrain.net/93/parkour-vs-freerunning.html

http://www.livestrong.com/article/538855-parkour-vs-freerunning/

Basics

http://www.livestrong.com/article/362784-parkour-jumping-and-leaping-tips/

http://www.livestrong.com/article/463144-basic-moves-that-traceurs-must-master-to-practice-freerunning-and-parkour/

Techniques

http://parkourpedia.com/technique/basic-balance

http://apexmovement.com/blog/top-10-bodyweight-exercises-for-intermediate-parkour-practitioners/

http://www.askmen.com/sports/bodybuilding_150/175b_fitness_tip.htm

Movements

http://news.discovery.com/adventure/extreme-sports/parkour-for-beginners-5-moves-you-can-master-quickly.htm

https://www.youtube.com/user/TappBrothers/videos

Exercises and Conditioning

http://www.nerdfitness.com/blog/2010/08/12/the-definitive-guide-to-parkour-for-beginners/

http://www.apexmovement.com/blog/how-to-start-parkour-a-beginners-guide/

Made in the USA
San Bernardino, CA
05 January 2019